preverbs

from behind

comes up

scorned beauty

preverbs

George Quasha

Between Editions

Between Editions are published by Station Hill of Barrytown, 120 Station Hill Road, Barrytown, NY 12507, as a project of The Institute for Publishing Arts, Inc., a not-for-profit, Federally tax-exempt organization, 501(c)(3), in Barrytown, New York.

www.stationhill.org

Designed by Susan Quasha in collaboration with the author
Front cover: Axial Drawing from the Dakini Series [#1, 11-6-11, 42"x47"] by George Quasha

ISBN: 978-1-58177-128-2

Printed in the United States of America

for Roger Woolger

from behind

comes up

scorned beauty

holding true

A forest without trees turns color musically.

There is a logic that does not follow itself.

Today I can't resist telling the world, *hold on, trees are ears, earth hears.*

Now I'm thinking *engineer nothing*—the coming moment's here on the other side.

I write what I can't yet think.

What say today sides with poetic quest by not stopping to question.

Keep an ear to the ground, it is said, even now, even here, listening soft.

It pulls the tongue back until the canopy opens.

Speech originates.

Beauty comes to out of the blue.

The name she thinks colors her perception.

To save her you strip away the cover.

The stem grips inside.

As I read her body flashes through the line, slash to syllabic slash.

Last things in the middle is an involuntary peep show.

Origin is intransitive.

The poem has no outside on its own.

I'm hunting down my transgressors, way inside here, syllable by syllable.

I want to see the face in retention.

Did the Drunken Boat throw the poet at wave peak?

It teaches *to lie down in darkness* is understanding *not*.

No one knows how to read poetry.

It knows itself before you.

The faces coming from inside rime young in the heart chime.

Restart. The dream translates its unthinkable domains.

Rescanning relinks lost layers.

3 *sensory things can make no sense*

Vision has no outside but runs through the body.

Sleeping beauty dreams it is a woman.

Slowing down mind shows its true colors.

You hear the forest reconfiguring before your eyes.

Truth shows in the logic that does not follow itself.

Wild waves bring out the wild rider.

Thus my fingers do the work of the mouth as it is reading.

Looking for signs of wisdom between words releases.

Meaning is what is retained without benefit of memory.

The line does not recall predecessors yet crosses the same streams.

My mouth remembers being a woman.

Mind slows to seethrough trees flashing by.

It makes you want to go over to the other side of yourself.

The mouth remembers what the rest of me forgot.

It thinks from the inside into any other inside.

Life intensifies at cross-purposes.

This is my best outside.

Connections sense at a distance.

I'm picking up on the raging beast in the esophageal sense.

Everything knows where it is although it has forgotten.

The voice in retention gets through almost anything over time.

Patience, that it discover its attractions, retained in sound itself.

Wild words come back through in waves.

Look on over.

It sounds itself.

This is a crossing point where anything I think weighs differently going further.

I long to locate dead center in every utterance.

Finding out how to talk Lazarus into rising has its poetics.

Awakened words historicize whenever you open your mouth.

Obviously nothing is obvious.

The commonplace is what undoes itself most secretly.

The same is yet to come.

Now breaking word is out of its corral.

It teaches to mean through an alien door.

Surrendering the leaf to the tree I understand *under* and *stand.*

Now I scare easy. All this is happening very close.

The perspectival nature of history is a word thing.

Exact sensorial simulacra impregnate the gaps between.

Last things in the middle, first things last.

I grow raw all over.

Every moment here is looking around its corner.

The mind can't help registering rotten.

I find myself the fool folded in.

I feel the rhythm pulsing watching its feet.

This is how I know where I am.

My past is gone on.

I'm found forth.

The present known is surprise itself.

Saying *true world* is not to know what is said.

Between these thoughts I think to see original nature.

Rose saying its other has only to say *rose*.

Nothing teaches but saying itself.

7 *time to pack*

I've come to be your follower.

Without you I'm not here.

No voice not hearing can still be heard.

Life is struggling to hear what it says. *I work here.*

For my part I labor to do what I'm told.

Finding it hard to get around big mind is still going around.

Time passing means it's harder to know I'm me.

I know speaking moving on.

It can't help taking itself personally but it soon forgets.

Still recall not knowing what anything means, the familiar is yet to come.

Returning here the same is saying what is never said.

3:33 AM primes time and nothing else or less.

A slight shift in tone color initiates the next world.

Anything is never heard before when really heard at all.

Let's get straight that hating cute is not hating the child.

Ideas have you from nowhere.

It's what fate would be if in the longrun it actually survived poetics.

Aiming to not aim leaves me at this crossroads and its devil of a fix.

I resort to poetry to watch what I say.

True caesura is loss of moment, my language is turning in.

Yes/no, same thing, *Pallaksch, Pallaksch!*, with slight hesitation to float right.

Reading 5 books at once finds the 5 channels to breathe through confluent.

Reading like incarnation's not here to purify, here to conflate—be co-blown through.

Necessity in time is the call to unnecessary complexity, naturally.

Beauty comes to [lost moment] out of the blue.

If the center didn't find itself on center all the lines would float away in space.

9 *view from the carpet*

I'm only ever speaking to one person, you.

I paint your portrait please.

Tell me if you know me.

The mirror is itself reflecting further.

I can't bear not being spoken in.

A whole life of clearing ears, seers.

It's high here.

You want to touch in total in this instant appearing.

The world is alluring through self-deflection.

You want more and *behold* it is more.

Had the center lost its center I'd have whirled away in space, no poem.

It returns on my own carpet.

The view is everywhere it goes everywhere.

10 *abide on by*

I didn't come here to say who I am.

If I knew who was speaking I'd tell.

I live in the crack from which it leaks.

It thinks I'm crazy—speaking pronominally.

Language floats as free as let.

It's only human, except when it isn't.

Speak the flower through.

There *you* are, I know because I'm speaking.

How not to love your unreal outside.

Anyway possible to squeeze out of the feeling of wasting life.

Killing two birds with the one to let both live accordingly. The twist.

Gesture sharpens to the pen's point.

Time to tie my shoelaces and thought strands at once.

11 *time on paper is flat*

The poem knows it can't find out who it is.

On the surface I don't know any one-surface people.

Knowing you are born pronominal opens you to your splits.

Intrinsic paradox comes down to saying anything true at all.

I watch the effort trying to have ears for the world.

The discourse is such that the distinction *lie* is always premature.

Can you tell when you're just playing at incarnation?

Times when the rock-a-bye-baby universe drops you you fall free.

The high path of giving up nothing.

On second thought I wasn't born.

Fuck paradox.

No point. I still feel the breeze of aftermath.

To detach, squeeze.

Haunting by request, unthinkable things are tracking down the right word.

There is a poetics of thinking true wherein truth has no contrary.

A sentence is language doing what it's told—fate, right before your eyes.

Each word spoken tries to tell its story.

Middle things come first.

The non-liar's paradox is truer.

There are alternative ways of being on the level.

One way claims its real estate like knowing the scent of its kind.

Head word talks its way off the left margin claiming physical space here.

A *thought has its music to complete in the saaaying, as trees sway here.*

Speaking is consequential as history is perspectival, therefore what.

The curtain goes up on the speaking that makes all this inevitable.

The poem calls the one friend who can take you back from yourself.

I'm waving to you in a fly-by.

I'll know I'm home as a line knows its place in the poem.

The mother tongue repairs syllable by syllable.

It's got me by the throat.

I'm rounding you up to prove you're as many as me.

Sound from center line voices a call to go on.

There's a hearing one and all or not at all.

Each syllable she lets loose magnetizes the book.

Proof by poetics is basic to the nothing that binds us so firm.

The art is fly-by-night. So let go.

Not knowing my whereabouts is the non-starter that brings us here.

As for *who*abouts how deny we've found each other having gotten this far?

Read my lips poem (her tongue engraves) presses me still as the line folds back.

It's fall and this place is all.

Watch it play my disappearance while sound winds back.

Nature or word it nurtures when heard.

Healing by laying on of lips writes its flipbook in the flesh.

Incarnate flaws fall out from not knowing who you are.

You've got your ear to a barrel while the whale breaches farther than who.

Residues, lost proverbs of soma, voluntary hauntings, what say but can't resist.

The same old twist there before you is neither same nor old. Nor you.

Do less.

Douse with forced ventricular flow lines, turbulent half-sensed sublime rip.

I take my hat off to senseless simple sensible things, although they ignore me.

I let it take my pulse then ride.

This is said to be the setup: *The flip frees in the fall, flawlessly.*

15 *avoiding zen frenzy in silence*

I am he who has to be here for no good reason.

The phrase *bed of longing* played through mind with no apparent referent.

The mouth opens and mind sees into the flow forth vibratory object in array.

Each syllable imagines its time—at my expense.

If it's said here it's *first* even if I think I know it.

My horse with scorn in her name always comes in ahead of herself from behind.

The poem is true in having to be. As I have to be.

There's something known only in the instant before the starting gate bell rings.

The text shows intestinal pressure.

It turns out.

Or he who has to be as I am I am.

The going discourse rescans in situ at the peak of fold back. Open middle.

On the high-charge track each entity steps up to teach its own new basic reading.

Intelligence finds new places to hide between words.

Sounds hover to recover—joiners hanging with coiners.

Saying readies by day, spreads wide by night.

Amor fati—love in the lay of human say.

Now is the heart of aware.

Got drunk one night and left my craft in the port of nowhere.

She was right proud I called her by her names of scorn.

Her crown of thorns from moment born gave culture. *Now whirl.*

As the hero crosses over I am he who overhears her unheard lives.

Life intelligence finds new ways to abide between hives.

Hence this past-hive therapy reaching for the life switch as we speak.

Born bitch to the tune of the abiding itch. *Whirl on.*

These strung lines of vibratory integrity only seem to circle.

Tuning is circulation.

The next step is crossing.

Looking for the following falls off the felt track where I hear her trace.

There's a cry in there that won't leave me listening.

The string rhythms audible only after layering down through sentenced ejections.

Making love in the lacunae's sheer joy in the thick removal nowhere.

I dropped off my symbols at recycling.

On the way I'm back with element thanks to elementals.

Power is pointing at the crossing.

What hits hardest is barely pronominal.

How can I throw you a hand across these vast intimacies?

The matrices of possible reframing a line at a time, keeping time to wild birds.

Lingual action at a distance shakes open blocks before dying.

18 *fuel at crossing sitting clear*

Hovering at the margin of sleep upright teaches dying reading.

I'm not half me as they take me back across.

Keeping feet on the ground holding on to my hat I let my head go on over.

What you are reading I am reading to you from half there.

The voice keeps trying to say reality into its tripped through undisclosed accuracy.

*Dis*array—how it shows up falling out from itself.

I find my voice in an unfamiliar disposal unit wondering how did it get there.

Gut wisdom teaches in belly laughs to throw its oracular vocals all the way across.

Listening backtracks syntax in the fateful saying going on.

The gentlest accuracy all the way down to elementals is merciless.

I am being given, if I may venture the expression, birth into death.

We are alienated most familially who live ventriloquilly.

The feet are clear already, of the great cunt of existence, Malone continues.

19 *echoic bardoics*

I turn into my favorite hideaway on this long self-pacing walkabout talk.

Sound waves surface under me is how I'd say I say in this time framed.

Follow the bouncing syllable. Dirigible.

I turn into a green black hawk in my dream of reaching you here in talk.

Time to cross the line, she's asking for it.

Sentence deflowers in switch words. Error, terror, arrow.

Gastromancy is midway in the journey doing talkabout at a distance.

I rub the word three times, lips aflame.

Poem is thinking into language.

Magic matters midthroat.

Dying is living back through.

Nothing I say is twice true thenceforth through and through.

It's my poem when it teaches me to read from scratch.

I'm reading my friend's further mind still passing over in this writing.

How personal to be the blank attractor that calls released psyche across your spot.

I bathe in the divide, almost reaching overall veiling away.

On the line prioritizes being heard by what no longer can be seen.

Leaving his body leaves me free of a me going right along.

He sheds a skin for me.

He's letting be said only what cannot not be said.

Fateful saying true to the root has no known listening but inevitable living.

He's waiting for the tone that cuts you loose—the poem of the voice to come.

Even the long full life remains to be said, the calling out in vanishing here.

Jointure heats in the release, friction in the slide through, down, around.

Dream life remembers itself as recalled by destination, rounding, torsional.

Life says *gone* in the tone I hear in *gong*.

There's a sense of life that has no contrary.

Still. I can't talk with you now in that other room.

The particular aphasia that grants access requires ever further redescription.

I thee inscribe by the other further mothering return.

come in come in [] ***Roger out and over***

I write you back across to right the loss on track.

I get tired and let you sound me over to the other sounding down under.

The great intimacy suddenly spreads her forked tongues.

I am living the other lives faster than the speed of thought.

Faster than speeding desire, blazing oblivious to oblivion. Wakening.

Entering another awake. Finally I begin to know you as you cannot know yourself.

Adding on by subtraction the inner torque's traction is *I don't understand language*.

No use for it now but that it use me here to bear its further other.

SUB-CONTENTS

scorned beauty comes up from behind

George Quasha's poetry includes *Somapoetics* (1973), *Giving the Lily Back Her Hands* (1979), *Ainu Dreams* (1999), and *Verbal Paradise (preverbs)* (2011). *Preverbs* has been a core vehicle for over a decade and is currently structured as seven books, each with seven poem-complexes. The present work is a poem-complex from the sixth book, *Exchanging Intentions (preverbs)*, yet to be published.

His work, exploring principles in common within various mediums in addition to language, includes sculpture, drawing, video, sound, installation, and performance, and his book *Axial Stones: An Art of Precarious Balance*, Foreword by Carter Ratcliff (2006), presents his work in axial sculpture, along with axial drawing and language. His work has been exhibited at the Baumgartner Gallery (New York), Slought Foundation (Philadelphia), the Samuel Dorsky Museum of Art (SUNY New Paltz), the Snite Museum of Art (Notre Dame), and elsewhere.

The internationally exhibited video work *art is: Speaking Portraits* records over 900 artists, poets, and musicians in eleven countries (saying what art/music/poetry is). Awarded a Guggenheim Fellowship in video art and an NEA Fellowship in poetry, he is the author (with Charles Stein) of *An Art of Limina: Gary Hill's Works and Writings* (foreword by Lynne Cooke) (2009). The anthology *America a Prophecy: A New Reading of American Poetry from Pre-Columbian Times to the Present*, co-edited with Jerome Rothenberg in 1973, is being reissued by Station Hill of Barrytown (SHP Archive Editions), of which he is co-founder/-publisher with Susan Quasha. He performs both solo and in collaboration with Gary Hill, Charles Stein, and David Arner.

Continuing work appears at www.quasha.com.

This publication includes
34 numbered copies of a limited, signed edition,
including an original drawing.

Special thanks to
Susan Quasha
for the design of text and cover
using an axial drawing from the Dakini Series
by George Quasha.

The text was set in Electra,
with Centaur and Apolline titling.